Banastre Tarleton's cavalrymen in a skirmish in January, 1781

COVER: *George Washington in John Trumbull's painting,* The Battle of Princeton.
YALE UNIVERSITY ART GALLERY

FRONT ENDSHEET: *Alexander Hamilton's forces overrun the redcoats at Yorktown.*
VIRGINIA STATE CAPITOL

CONTENTS PAGE: *A detail from* The Battle of Princeton, *by William Mercer.*
HISTORICAL SOCIETY OF PENNSYLVANIA

BACK ENDSHEET: The Surrender of Yorktown, *by Louis Van Blarenberghe, 1784.*
MUSEE DE VERSAILLES, PARIS

"A knowledge of the past prepares us for the crisis of the present and the challenge of the future."

JOHN F. KENNEDY
From his special foreword in Volume 1

THE AMERICAN HERITAGE NEW ILLUSTRATED HISTORY OF THE UNITED STATES

VOLUME 3

THE REVOLUTION

By ROBERT G. ATHEARN
Professor of History, University of Colorado

CREATED AND DESIGNED BY THE EDITORS OF
AMERICAN HERITAGE
The Magazine of History

PUBLISHED BY
DELL PUBLISHING CO., INC., NEW YORK

CONTENTS OF THE COMPLETE SERIES

Foreword by JOHN F. KENNEDY
Introduction by ALLAN NEVINS
Main text by ROBERT G. ATHEARN

A COMPLETE INDEX FOR ALL 16 VOLUMES APPEARS IN VOLUME 16

© 1963 by American Heritage Publishing Co., Inc., 551 Fifth Avenue, New York 17, New York. All rights reserved
under Berne and Pan-American Copyright Conventions. Library of Congress Catalogue Card Number: 63–11118.

CONTENTS OF VOLUME 3

CHAPTER 7

Rabble in arms

The Continental Association, framed at the meeting of the First Continental Congress in the fall of 1774, was no mere oratorical expression of resistance against England. It was the beginning of a struggle for independence. America, from Massachusetts to Georgia, was united as never before in a series of pledges to protect the rights of the colonies.

If those on this side of the Atlantic recognized the seriousness of the situation, George III did not. Stubbornly he told his prime minister, Lord North, that a state of rebellion existed, and that, while Britain yielded not an inch, "blows must decide whether they are to be subject to this country or independent." To his surprise, the colonials met his challenge.

During the winter of 1774–75, antagonism between British troops and the colonials heightened. While General Thomas Gage concentrated his troops around Boston, neighboring villagers, angered by the threat of military action, quietly gathered pow-

American patriots, full of the feeling of their independence, pull down the statue of George III in New York in July, 1776.

der and ball. Gage learned from his spies that in the village of Concord, 21 miles from Boston, there was a major supply depot, and that in Lexington, five miles from Concord, there were a couple of incendiaries named Samuel Adams and John Hancock.

After some temporizing, Gage dispatched 700 soldiers to capture the two men and destroy the supplies. As Gage's men marched on the evening of April 18, William Dawes and, later, Paul Revere pounded on horseback through the night to warn of the redcoats' advance. The alarm sounded, the colonials turned out, and when Gage's troops appeared in Lexington at dawn, they were met by 70 villagers in military formation. In the ensuing exchange of shots, eight Americans died and 10 were wounded. Leaving the rebels to count their losses, His Majesty's troops now moved on to Concord. The first blood in the American Revolution had been drawn.

After the supplies in Concord were destroyed, Gage's troops began the return march. The brush at Lexington now proved to be more serious than they had thought. Angry farmers all over the area snatched rifles from

General Thomas Gage was commander of the British forces in America, 1763–1775.

above their fireplaces and swarmed after the red line. Under fire, the British troops stumbled along, men falling dead with frightening regularity. When 1,500 reinforcements with two fieldpieces arrived, the fighting sharpened. By night the British were safe in Cambridge, but the journey to Concord had cost them 247 in killed and wounded. The American "rabble," who were not supposed to be a match for the king's men, had lost 88.

A time for decision

The encounter at Lexington and Concord was of no great military significance, yet it was a symbol to colonials. Lord North's government had already begun to relax certain restrictions, but fast-moving events nullified his conciliating efforts. The king, upon hearing from General Gage, said firmly that "America must be a colony of England or treated as an enemy." Americans all along the Atlantic Coast were equally angered by the affair. In Virginia, George Washington announced that now it was either war or slavery. In South Carolina, two regiments of troops were easily formed. During these heated days, delegates to the Second Continental Congress were traveling toward Philadelphia, where they would meet on May 10, 1775.

The skirmish in the Massachusetts villages now became a flaming challenge, and because of it the delegates to the Second Continental Congress were faced with new and perplexing problems. They had talked merely of resistance the year before; now they were called upon to decide more dangerous questions. Their very existence was revolutionary. The home government had prohibited them even from meeting, and their assembling was in direct violation of the law. Resolved to proceed under any circumstances, they began their sessions. Soon it was apparent that delegates from all the colonies were in favor of supporting Massachusetts in her time of need. Although the delegates denied any plans for independence, they stood by the rights of the colonies to resist what they regarded as oppression.

When the Continental Army was formed, and Washington placed at its head, Congress justified the action by publishing a declaration setting forth "the Causes and Necessities of Taking Up Arms." Independence was not mentioned. But the document's words sounded ominously like it: "Our cause is just. Our union is perfect. Our internal resources are great. . . ." Despite the strength of the moderates in the gathering, the force of circumstance would propel Americans down the road to independence. Perhaps they did not know it, but they had passed the point of no return.

The Battle of Bunker Hill

Already fate was setting in place the combustibles of final separation. General Gage, now reinforced, resolved to strengthen his fortifications around Boston by occupying nearby heights. He began his movements in mid-June of 1776, and was at once answered by Massachusetts militiamen, who dug in atop Breed's Hill. British warships in the harbor lobbed shells at the militiamen while infantry units stormed their position. Twice the British were driven off, but on the third assault they routed the Americans, whose powder supply had been exhausted. Thus the battle, misnamed after adjacent Bunker Hill, ended. It was neither a great victory for the British nor a signal defeat for the Americans. But the fact of the battle was significant, for it indicated to the British that there was growing in America a determination to fight. Many along the Atlantic seaboard were thrilled by this example of American armed resistance to the overwhelming power of England.

The day before Bunker Hill, George

Paul Revere was painted at his silversmith's workbench by John Singleton Copley.

Washington accepted from the Continental Congress command of the Continental Army at Philadelphia; by early July he was at Cambridge ready for active duty. Here he found a mob of approximately 16,000 men, mostly from Massachusetts. Soon Congress supplied him with 3,000 more from the middle colonies. All in all, it was a strange array. There were no uniforms; shades of brown and green stood out among multicolored clothing. Washington suggested that hunting shirts be worn "to unite the men and abolish those provincial distinctions." Officers were elected by their men, a custom to continue for some time in the American armed forces, and rather than demand the privileges of rank, many officers even did somewhat menial tasks to gain their men's favor. Among the

officers of highest rank, commissioned by Congress, there were dissatisfactions; each felt he was entitled to a position of greater importance and responsibility. General Washington had little to make him optimistic as he set forth to bring order out of chaos.

The house divided

Events like Lexington and Concord, followed by the larger battle at Breed's Hill, cut sharply through the strata of American society. Many men who previously had accepted things as they were now had to declare themselves for or against independence. Conservatives and, in general, those who held offices in America struggled to maintain the connection with England. They angered those who regarded war as the only course, and with each violent incident the breach widened. Radical leaders like Sam Adams, who had urged independence for nearly a decade, seized upon the division and fanned the flames of revolution to white heat. Another firebrand, Thomas Paine, published his pamphlet *Common Sense,* and at once it became a best seller. The propagandist, as always, had put into words what many men had been thinking but could not say.

The British seemed continually to

With some of their men bareheaded and wounded, the British troops form into columns and to the sound of drums march stoically across the trampled grass and up Breed's Hill—in a painting by Howard Pyle.

provide reasons for colonial charges against them. The king had already announced that blows must decide the issue, and when he received what was called the Olive Branch Petition from the colonies, he rejected it, stigmatizing all Americans as disloyal. The moderate William Pitt proposed a compromise, but Parliament rejected it. In October, 1775, the Continental Congress learned that Falmouth, Maine, had been burned by a British naval force, and three months later Norfolk, Virginia, was razed. Each occurrence underscored the charges of men like Sam Adams and Tom Paine that King George was not infallible and that perhaps he was a "royal brute" after all. Inevitably the road led toward revolution.

The declaration

As early as April, 1776, Richard Henry Lee, head of a great Virginia family, advised Patrick Henry that immediate independence was a necessity because the home government had placed the colonies in a position of anarchy. Here was a man whose sons were then at school in England, whose brother was an official in London, and whose own living came from the sale of tobacco in English markets. Yet he saw no alternative to taking the extreme step.

Not everyone agreed with him. But a month later, on May 15, Virginia passed resolutions, saying their delegates to Congress ought to propose independence. And on June 7, Lee offered a resolution that the colonies were free and independent states, having no further allegiance to Great Britain. But Congress, like most groups, had its conservatives, and they were opposed to declaring a state of independence. Edward Rutledge of South Carolina led the opposition, which argued that to take a position before doing anything to maintain it was foolish.

About all the conservatives could do was gain a delay of three weeks. During the last days of June, while the debate continued, Lee's fellow Virginian, Thomas Jefferson, along with Benjamin Franklin, John Adams, Roger Sherman, and Robert B. Livingston, worked out a draft of an independence declaration. And on July 2, Congress passed the Lee resolution that the American colonies were independent of England. John Adams predicted that the date would "be celebrated by succeeding generations as the great anniversary Festival." But it was not. July 4, when the amended and revised declaration was approved, was to become the anniversary date.

The Declaration of Independence was not intended to be in any sense radical. Jefferson himself said he did not attempt to incorporate anything new or startling, that he simply tried to present "an expression of the American mind." There were two main parts to the Declaration—a preamble and a catalogue of grievances. It was in the preamble that Jefferson and his associates turned to the writings of

190

John Locke, an English political philosopher, in search of a general justification for what they were about to do. They borrowed so heavily from Locke that they even used several of his phrases. The heart of their argument was that "all men are created equal, that they are endowed by their Creator with certain inalienable Rights; that among them are Life, Liberty, and the pursuit of Happiness." Thus paraphrasing a writer well known to Americans of their day, Jefferson and the others sketched out the right of revolution under certain conditions of oppression. It was their contention that if the British government was unwilling to grant a portion of its subjects the rights they considered basic, those so denied might, with justification, break away.

The second main part of the Decla-

The British swarm over Breed's Hill in their third assault as the American Major John Pitcairn (right), mortally wounded, is carried from the field, and patriot Dr. Joseph Warren (left) dies. The painting is by John Trumbull.

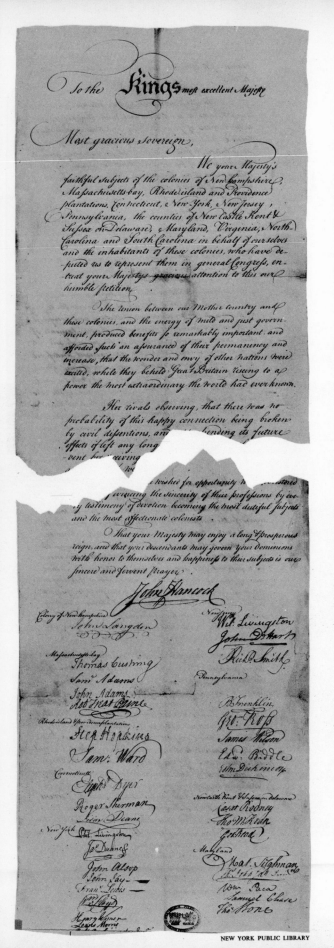

ration was a bill of particulars stating why the American move for independence was a necessity. The list was a long one, aimed at the king, who was accused of all manner of injustices to the colonials. It was meant to arouse Americans and bring sympathy from those in England who did not like George III. The indictment against him referred to the dissolution of colonial legislatures, the hindrance of immigration, the packing of government offices in America, the "illegal" quartering of troops in the colonies, and the imposition of taxes without the consent of those taxed. The authors of the Declaration concluded this portion of their indictment with the comment that George III was "unfit to be the ruler of a free People." The only reference to Parliament was the statement that the Americans had warned their British cousins "of attempts by their legislature to extend an unwarrantable jurisdiction over us." In conclusion, the signatories declared the independence of the American colonies from Great Britain and a total dissolution of any and all previous connections with the crown.

None of the charges got to the root of the matter. Perhaps not even Jefferson could have done so. The alienation had come about so gradually that few could isolate the real reasons for discontent. Jefferson would have had to describe the history of each of the col-

The Olive Branch Petition, as John Adams named it, was flatly rejected by George III.

onies from its original grant of political powers. He might have pointed out that conservatives tended to stay home and liberals tended to migrate, thus weighting the population in America with those inclined to independence. But such reasons were general and intangible. They would not have been convincing to those who were to take up the struggle and carry it on. This is perhaps why Jefferson dealt with specific and recent, if somewhat unsupportable, charges of mistreatment at the hands of the king.

Uniting the states

A few days after its approval by Congress, the Declaration was publicly read in Philadelphia, the seat of the newborn government. John Adams wrote that there was great and boisterous rejoicing. "The bells rang all day and almost all night." Before long it was read in other colonies, too, with the same reaction.

The writing and promulgation of the Declaration proved to be a master stroke on the part of those in Congress who had strongly supported independence. Now it was too late to turn back. A new nation had been born, and even those who had clung to the hope of remaining a part of the Empire were obliged to support it or suffer the consequences. That the sentiment was fixed in writing and that its supporters had signed it seemed to legalize it and make it permanent.

Although the Declaration provided the emergent nation with clear-cut

Patrick Henry

war aims from the outset, many showed little enthusiasm for violence. These conservatives, who mostly had been associated with the Tories, recoiled from such a radical step as civil war. To be sure, many of them resented England's regulatory legislation, but the home government indisputably represented law and order. Being property holders, they wanted England's protection for their holdings. More than once she had intervened to save aristocratic colonials from the demands of the common people. Judging the present situation, the conservatives concluded it was safer to put up with Parliament, with all its restrictions, than to consort

193

with the democratic experimenters.

At the time of the Declaration of Independence, perhaps one-third of the colonial population could be counted as loyalist. The group included officeholders, members of the Anglican church, and the military. Not only did they have a high regard for the authority of the crown, but they were unwilling to cut all ties with the past in favor of a new and untried venture. They had no assurance that the result would be no more than a break with England. Revolutions often get out of hand, and should social upheaval accompany political change, men of property and high position would be the losers. About 60,000 loyalists left the colonies, electing not to take their chances with more daring Americans. Other thousands, who did not want to leave, quietly turned over their property to friends or relatives who were regarded favorably by the revolutionaries and sat out the storm, saying nothing.

The "patriots," or what might be called the Popular Party, were a mixture of radicals and men who simply went along, often reluctantly. The fighting core of this body found its strength in the left wing of the Whig Party in America and represented a triumph of the liberals over the conservatives. Many a man like John Dickinson, who opposed the move for independence, fought alongside his fellow Americans when the time for shooting came. Dickinson, a well-known colonial leader, humbly joined the Continental Army as a private.

The Popular Party was also diverse in the origins of its members. There were small farmers, artisans, frontiersmen, free-trade merchants, and even well-to-do Southern planters. The planters contributed Thomas Jefferson, George Mason, and, for a while, Patrick Henry. Most of them had no intention of participating in a movement that might develop along democratic lines. They felt that property must be protected, the rights of gentlemen preserved, and class status recognized. "We are not contending that our rabble or all unqualified persons shall have the right of voting," said one Southerner. With this in mind, the landed gentry guided the Revolution as a movement against England and closed their ears to talk about dividing the spoils when the fighting was over. So well did they accomplish their purpose of focusing the struggle on grievances against the mother country that the "revolution from within" was not fully recognized until after 1782.

War propaganda

In exciting their fellow Americans against the British Empire, propagandists on this side of the Atlantic did a first-rate job. All the weaknesses and corruptions of the mother country were dragged out to make her appear decadent and cruel and to be sucking the life out of the colonies in order to save herself. Americans were warned repeatedly that if they remained in the Empire, they would "see their property used to glut the avarice of half a million swag-bellied pensioners" in England. America of 1775 was made to appear as the virtuous child, obliged to support a bankrupt and profligate parent. Alexander Hamilton estimated that it would take Britain 120 years to pay off her existing debt provided she did not go to war, and he was sure there would be no such reign of peace. It was his firm belief that England's next war would be her last.

In England, meanwhile, there was a tendency to discount both the intentions and capabilities of the Americans. Propagandists worked hard to present the colonials as shaggy squirrel hunters, totally undisciplined and even lacking in courage. As the hardcore revolutionaries were descendants of Englishmen who had left home to brave the trials of life in the wilds of America, questioning their courage

seemed hardly supportable. That it was an error would be proved again and again during the war. Others who discounted the chances of American success pointed out that there was no unity among the colonials. Here they were on stronger ground. Differences between the North and the South already were apparent, and those who doubted that they could be reconciled even in war were not far from right. The differences would be one of the major problems facing the leaders.

Propagandists on both sides were playing to an audience larger than at home. Anxious eyes were cast toward the Continent, for there lay the balance of power. Englishmen wanted no interference in what they regarded as a domestic disturbance, while Americans openly solicited foreign aid. France and Spain were the most likely to interfere. France still felt the pain of having nearly all her American co-

The Maryland Regiment leaves Annapolis on July 10, 1776, to join Washington.

lonial holdings taken by the British in 1763. Ever since, she had competed fiercely with the British, particularly in the Caribbean sugar islands, and her interest in transatlantic holdings had not died. Concurrently, Spain and England were at swords' points over commercial rivalries and had come nearly to blows in 1770. Both France and Spain yearned for a chance to strike at the proud mistress of the seas. They realized she got part of her strength from the thriving commerce of her American colonies, and in the hope of cutting it off, they listened to all the revolutionaries had to say.

Strategy of war

Regardless of propaganda, there *were* some long-range considerations. The British were faced by difficulties greater than they would admit. The land where they proposed to fight was over 3,000 miles away, and their opponent was skilled in warfare. Moreover, sympathy for America was so great in England that Hessian troops had to be hired to fight the colonials.

Although 15,000 or more troops were usually available in Great Britain, there were fewer than 5,000 in the fall of 1775. A large part of the British army was in America or the West Indies. The most effective force was the 9,000 men in Boston, but for the moment General Washington had them cornered. Americans controlled the Atlantic coastline. And capture of the major seaports would not quell the rebellion. The British would have to work inland, foot by foot, and subdue the rebels as they found them. But supply lines would grow aggravatingly long and expensive to maintain and casualties would mount alarmingly with each mile of advance.

On the other hand, if the Americans were as united as the Declaration of Independence suggested, they should have won their war in much less time. Despite such announcements of union, American individualism was never more than briefly submerged, and it would bob to the surface in quarrels among states, jealousies between sections, and in man-to-man bickering. Few wanted to serve in the Continental Army, and those who did often gave but a few months of their time. In America of 1776 there was a natural hostility to a large regular army. The struggle became a militiaman's war, with small groups turning out to fight under the leadership of some local officer like Francis Marion. Then, when the area was freed from immediate danger of invasion, the men went back to planting corn and haying. While they were willing to fight for their own communities, most colonials showed little interest in defending others. Thus, although several hundred thousand men may have participated in the war, few took part continuously or for long periods. Washington's army, at its peak of 18,000 in early 1776, fell to fewer than 5,000 before the war was over. It was enough to discourage the most hopeful of leaders.

THE
DECLARATION
OF
INDEPENDENCE

The famous event that Americans celebrate every Fourth of July was the formal beginning of the American Revolution. But the Declaration of Independence was more than a declaration of war. It was the first great document in the history of a nation whose name would come to be a symbol of freedom to all the world. The men who adopted it did not feel it to be anything new or radical in principle, for it expressed ideas that had become common property to leading minds of the 18th century. Yet it *was* new in announcing those ideas as the basis of an actual society. Its foundation was the theory of natural rights—ones to which all men were entitled simply by reason of being human, and which could not justly be taken from them: "Life, Liberty, and the pursuit of Happiness." From this followed logically the function of government, which was to make those rights more secure to every individual, by means of laws having the consent of the governed. But the Declaration marked the point of no return for the Revolution; it was not just a chapter in the history of ideas. The picture portfolio that follows illustrates some of the persons, places, and things associated with the dawning of the democratic epoch in the climactic summer of 1776.

1 The Draw Bridge 7 Jo
2 Bowe Building 8 Ca
3 Edw. Shipen' 9 Gr
4 Ant. Morris Brew Hou 10 Iro
5 Capt. Vining' 11 W
6 Jonathan Dickinson 12 Th

CRADLE OF REVOLUTION

Colonial Philadelphia is seen from the Delaware River in the pre-Revolution painting above. The many ships and substantial houses attest to the young city's metropolitan status. It was the most enterprising commercial center of America.

The building in Philadelphia where the Declaration was adopted and signed looked as it is at the left when the Continental Congress met there in 1776. Known as the State House, it was not called Independence Hall for another 75 years.

Nothing did more to rally public opinion to the cause of independence than Tom Paine's pamphlet *Common Sense,* of which the title page is shown at the right. His fiery eloquence convinced thousands that, as he put it, " 'Tis time to part!"

OVERLEAF: A detail from John Trumbull's celebrated painting, showing John Adams, Roger Sherman, Robert Livingston, Thomas Jefferson, and Benjamin Franklin, all members of the drafting committee, as they present the Declaration to Congress.

YALE UNIVERSITY ART GALLERY

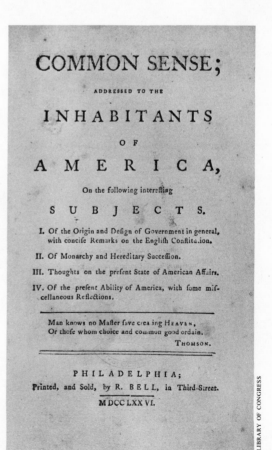

COMMON SENSE;

ADDRESSED TO THE

INHABITANTS

OF

AMERICA,

On the following interesting

SUBJECTS.

I. Of the Origin and Design of Government in general, with concise Remarks on the English Constitution.

II. Of Monarchy and Hereditary Succession.

III. Thoughts on the present State of American Affairs.

IV. Of the present Ability of America, with some miscellaneous Reflections.

Man knows no Master save creating HEAVEN,
Or those whom choice and common good ordain.
THOMSON.

PHILADELPHIA;
Printed, and Sold, by R. BELL, in Third-Street.
MDCCLXXVI.

LIBRARY OF CONGRESS

THE SPIRIT OF '76

ABBOT HALL

For the Centennial of the Declaration (right), Archibald M. Willard painted the scene that has come to symbolize the spirit of the Revolution. The disheartened Americans face defeat—until an indomitable trio of musicians rallies them to fight anew for the independence the Declaration has proclaimed.

IN CONGRESS, JULY 4, 1776.

The unanimous Declaration of the thirteen united States of America.

When in the Course of human events, it becomes necessary for one people to dissolve the political bands which have connected them with another, and to assume among the powers of the earth, the separate and equal station to which the Laws of Nature and of Nature's God entitle them, a decent respect to the opinions of mankind requires that they should declare the causes which impel them to the separation. — We hold these truths to be self-evident, that all men are created equal, that they are endowed by their Creator with certain unalienable Rights, that among these are Life, Liberty and the pursuit of Happiness. — That to secure these rights, Governments are instituted among Men, deriving their just powers from the consent of the governed, — That whenever any Form of Government becomes destructive of these ends, it is the Right of the People to alter or to abolish it, and to institute new Government, laying its foundation on such principles and organizing its powers in such form, as to them shall seem most likely to effect their Safety and Happiness. Prudence, indeed, will dictate that Governments long established should not be changed for light and transient causes; and accordingly all experience hath shewn, that mankind are more disposed to suffer, while evils are sufferable, than to right themselves by abolishing the forms to which they are accustomed. But when a long train of abuses and usurpations, pursuing invariably the same Object evinces a design to reduce them under absolute Despotism, it is their right, it is their duty, to throw off such Government, and to provide new Guards for their future security. — Such has been the patient sufferance of these Colonies; and such is now the necessity which constrains them to alter their former Systems of Government. The history of the present King of Great Britain is a history of repeated injuries and usurpations, all having in direct object the establishment of an absolute Tyranny over these States. To prove this, let Facts be submitted to a candid world. —

He has refused his Assent to Laws, the most wholesome and necessary for the public good. — He has forbidden his Governors to pass Laws of immediate and pressing importance, unless suspended in their operation till his Assent should be obtained; and when so suspended, he has utterly neglected to attend to them. — He has refused to pass other Laws for the accommodation of large districts of people, unless those people would relinquish the right of Representation in the Legislature, a right inestimable to them and formidable to tyrants only. — He has called together legislative bodies at places unusual, uncomfortable, and distant from the depository of their public Records, for the sole purpose of fatiguing them into compliance with his measures. — He has dissolved Representative Houses repeatedly, for opposing with manly firmness his invasions on the rights of the people. — He has refused for a long time, after such dissolutions, to cause others to be elected; whereby the Legislative powers, incapable of Annihilation, have returned to the People at large for their exercise; the State remaining in the mean time exposed to all the dangers of invasion from without, and convulsions within. — He has endeavoured to prevent the population of these States; for that purpose obstructing the Laws for Naturalization of Foreigners; refusing to pass others to encourage their migrations hither, and raising the conditions of new Appropriations of Lands. — He has obstructed the Administration of Justice, by refusing his Assent to Laws for establishing Judiciary powers. — He has made Judges dependent on his Will alone, for the tenure of their offices, and the amount and payment of their salaries. — He has erected a multitude of New Offices, and sent hither swarms of Officers to harass our people, and eat out their substance. — He has kept among us, in times of peace, Standing Armies without the Consent of our legislatures. — He has affected to render the Military independent of and superior to the Civil power. — He has combined with others to subject us to a jurisdiction foreign to our constitution, and unacknowledged by our laws; giving his Assent to their Acts of pretended Legislation: — For Quartering large bodies of armed troops among us: — For protecting them, by a mock Trial, from punishment for any Murders which they should commit on the Inhabitants of these States: — For cutting off our Trade with all parts of the world: — For imposing Taxes on us without our Consent: — For depriving us in many cases, of the benefits of Trial by Jury: — For transporting us beyond Seas to be tried for pretended offences: — For abolishing the free System of English Laws in a neighbouring Province, establishing therein an Arbitrary government, and enlarging its Boundaries so as to render it at once an example and fit instrument for introducing the same absolute rule into these Colonies: — For taking away our Charters, abolishing our most valuable Laws, and altering fundamentally the Forms of our Governments: — For suspending our own Legislatures, and declaring themselves invested with power to legislate for us in all cases whatsoever. — He has abdicated Government here, by declaring us out of his Protection and waging War against us. — He has plundered our seas, ravaged our Coasts, burnt our towns, and destroyed the lives of our people. — He is at this time transporting large Armies of foreign Mercenaries to compleat the works of death, desolation and tyranny, already begun with circumstances of Cruelty & perfidy scarcely paralleled in the most barbarous ages, and totally unworthy the Head of a civilized nation. — He has constrained our fellow Citizens taken Captive on the high Seas to bear Arms against their Country, to become the executioners of their friends and Brethren, or to fall themselves by their Hands. — He has excited domestic insurrections amongst us, and has endeavoured to bring on the inhabitants of our frontiers, the merciless Indian Savages, whose known rule of warfare, is an undistinguished destruction of all ages, sexes and conditions. In every stage of these Oppressions We have Petitioned for Redress in the most humble terms: Our repeated Petitions have been answered only by repeated injury. A Prince, whose character is thus marked by every act which may define a Tyrant, is unfit to be the ruler of a free people. Nor have We been wanting in attentions to our British brethren. We have warned them from time to time of attempts by their legislature to extend an unwarrantable jurisdiction over us. We have reminded them of the circumstances of our emigration and settlement here. We have appealed to their native justice and magnanimity, and we have conjured them by the ties of our common kindred to disavow these usurpations, which, would inevitably interrupt our connections and correspondence. They too have been deaf to the voice of justice and of consanguinity. We must, therefore, acquiesce in the necessity, which denounces our Separation, and hold them, as we hold the rest of mankind, Enemies in War, in Peace Friends. —

We, therefore, the Representatives of the united States of America, in General Congress, Assembled, appealing to the Supreme Judge of the world for the rectitude of our intentions, do, in the Name, and by Authority of the good People of these Colonies, solemnly publish and declare, That these United Colonies are, and of Right ought to be Free and Independent States; that they are Absolved from all Allegiance to the British Crown, and that all political connection between them and the State of Great Britain, is and ought to be totally dissolved; and that as Free and Independent States, they have full Power to levy War, conclude Peace, contract Alliances, establish Commerce, and to do all other Acts and Things which Independent States may of right do. — And for the support of this Declaration, with a firm reliance on the protection of Divine Providence, we mutually pledge to each other our Lives, our Fortunes and our sacred Honor.

Button Gwinnett
Lyman Hall
Geo Walton.

Wm Hooper
Joseph Hewes,
John Penn

Edward Rutledge.

Thos Heyward Junr.
Thomas Lynch Junr.
Arthur Middleton

John Hancock

Samuel Chase
Wm Paca
Thos Stone
Charles Carroll of Carrollton

George Wythe
Richard Henry Lee
Th Jefferson
Benj Harrison
Thos Nelson jr.
Francis Lightfoot Lee
Carter Braxton

Robt Morris
Benjamin Rush
Benj. Franklin
John Morton
Geo Clymer
Jas. Smith
Geo. Taylor
James Wilson
Geo. Ross
Caesar Rodney
Geo Read
Tho M:Kean

Wm Floyd
Phil. Livingston
Frans. Lewis
Lewis Morris

Richd Stockton
Jno Witherspoon
Fras. Hopkinson
John Hart
Abra Clark

Josiah Bartlett
Wm Whipple
Saml Adams
John Adams
Robt Treat Paine
Elbridge Gerry
Step Hopkins
William Ellery
Roger Sherman
Sam Huntington
Wm Williams
Oliver Wolcott
Matthew Thornton

THE DECISION IS MADE

HISTORICAL SOCIETY OF PENNSYLVANIA

On July 4, 1776, the Continental Congress, meeting in Independence Hall, solemnly voted that the Declaration of Independence be adopted. Robert Edge Pine and Edward Savage painted the scene above in 1785, nine years after the historic occasion. The courageous signers dipped their pens in the three-piece silver inkstand (right), still to be seen where they used it.

INDEPENDENCE NATIONAL HISTORICAL PARK, PHILADELPHIA

By mid-July most Americans had seen copies of the Declaration or heard it read in public. Above, an 18th-century print shows such a reading, and the listening crowd's reaction.

OVERLEAF: Parades, picnics, toasts, patriotic songs and declamations, fireworks—all these typical Fourth of July celebrations are seen in this 1819 painting by J. L. Krimmel.

CHAPTER 8

COCKPIT OF BATTLE

Military operations of some significance began before the signing of the Declaration of Independence on July 4, 1776. In the fall of 1775, the Americans invaded Canada, and on the last day of the year Generals Benedict Arnold and Richard Montgomery made an attack upon Quebec. Arnold, personally leading 650 of the men, moved past the gates and into the city, where he was met by gunfire that wounded a number of his soldiers and left a bullet in his own leg. Daniel Morgan, another of the American officers, found himself engaged in heavy street fighting and made the fatal mistake of holding up, waiting for assistance from Montgomery, who had been killed. The British counterattacked at this point, and house by house they drove back the Americans, forcing some to surrender and others to retreat. The price of the abortive assault was about 100 killed or wounded and perhaps 400 taken prisoner. With Arnold wounded and Montgomery dead, the campaign

The American leader Richard Montgomery dies during the 1775 attack on Quebec, in a detail from a John Trumbull painting.

was practically over. But the British, because of a raging snowstorm, did not take up a serious pursuit of the defeated remnants, nor did they drive the Americans out of Canada until the following spring. Although the thrust at Quebec was unsuccessful, it served to deter aggressive British moves from that direction at a critical time in the war. A large body of troops coming to America from England was diverted for the future defense of Quebec. To some Americans, however, the virtual destruction of a 5,000-man army and the large expenditure of money were a high price to pay for this kind of respite.

Patriots who read the discouraging news of failure at Quebec found solace in the dispatches from Boston. On the morning of March 26, 1776, Sir William Howe moved his army and about 1,000 Tory sympathizers out of that city. They sailed for Halifax, Nova Scotia, glad to be freed from the threatening American guns that peered down upon them from Dorchester Heights. During his confinement in Boston, Howe had pondered over ways to bring the colonial upstarts to heel. At first he thought a modest army, properly led, would do the job, but as time passed and reports of growing rebel strength came in, he gradually raised his estimates of the required number to about 20,000. New York, he decided, was the focal point, and after it was secured, the Hudson River would provide the means of driving a great wedge between New England and the other colonies.

The Southern campaign

The grand plan of divide and conquer would take time, particularly in view of the delays that Howe was encountering as he tried to refurbish his army at Halifax. New York was spared for the moment, while the Southern colonies absorbed the next British blows. As early as mid-1775, strategists across the Atlantic had convinced themselves and the king that only a few regulars were needed to bolster the loyalists from Virginia southward. Accordingly, in January, 1776, Sir Henry Clinton sailed from Boston with an expeditionary force, intending to join the loyalists at Cape Fear, North Carolina, from where the assault would be made. But before Clinton arrived, Governor Josiah Martin, too eager and confident, gave the word to attack, only to see his supporters instantly crushed by Colonel James Moore's militiamen. Those who fled, leaving behind their dead or wounded, were run down and captured, and Carolina's loyalist forces lost another 900 men.

Martin's precipitous action upset Clinton's plans, but after being joined by troops from England under Lord Cornwallis—with the support of Sir Peter Parker, whose fleet was anchored off Cape Fear—Clinton decided to try to take South Carolina and set out for Charleston. Congress, well aware that the slow-moving force was bound for a port of such importance, sought to prevent its capture. This busy harbor, perhaps the most vital along the Southern coastline, was a main base for privateers as well as a center of trade, and its loss would be serious. General Charles Lee was assigned to defend the Southern Department and hurried to his new post.

Colonel William Moultrie, a South Carolinian, was already preparing Charleston's defense, particularly the redoubts of Fort Moultrie on Sullivan's Island, which the invaders would have to pass to attack the city. Lee's demands that Moultrie abandon the fort, on the ground that it provided no avenue of retreat, and Moultrie's flat refusal to obey demonstrated an early conflict between central and state authority. When the British fleet appeared and bombarded Fort Moultrie for 12 hours, only to withdraw, leaving Charleston unscathed, it probably saved Moultrie some embarrassment. And Lee's mood must have become forgiving when he learned that a shot from shore had caught Admiral Parker in the posterior, tearing off the seat of his breeches and carrying away a patch of titled hide. Between the futility of the attack and Parker's

Benedict Arnold began his 350-mile march from Boston to Quebec with 1,100 men. He lost half to cold and hunger as he went through the wilds of Maine.

wounded dignity, the British decided to call it a day. Back to New York went Clinton, ready to aid Howe but determined to capture Charleston ultimately. Four years later he would.

Taking New York in 1776

To the British, New York was of more strategic importance than a city like Charleston, and with this the Americans agreed. Of the 25,000 residents in the spring of 1776, more than 10,000 labored to make Manhattan Island a graveyard for British landing forces. General Washington dispersed his forces among other islands in the harbor, determined to hold Manhattan at all costs. When, on July 2, 1776, Howe landed 10,000 men on Staten Island, there was no resistance, nor was there opposition as he built up his force to more than 30,000 in the following weeks. The Americans prepared their own defenses, hoping that an assault would be made as it had been at Breed's Hill, where the entrenched had the advantage. By mid-August they were getting restless,

211

unguarded. The woods around the Heights were thick with American riflemen, ready to shoot down the British and their Hessian mercenaries. But they never got the chance, for they were outflanked and struck savagely from behind. In panic they fled, and their pursuers pinned them to trees with bayonets as they futilely tried to reload their long rifles. Yet Washington got his men out of the near-disastrous situation and back to Manhattan, under cover of a heavy

Colonel William Moultrie (above), commander of the fort on Sullivan's Island outside of Charleston, gave the Americans a great victory in 1776 when his men withstood the attack of 10 British ships (right).

however, for the plodding, cautious Howe still had not made his move.

Because he wanted to winter his men on Manhattan, Howe was eager to capture it without unnecessary destruction. Yet until he forced the American artillery out of Brooklyn Heights, on Long Island, the city across the East River would be untenable for him. When he sent troops ashore on Long Island, there was again no resistance, as the Americans waited on the Heights. But the British had learned something in Boston, and this time they refused to fall into the trap. Instead of the main roads, they took ones that had been left

fog, because Howe did not follow up his advantage.

The respite was brief. During the next two months, British pressure against Manhattan forced another retreat, this time across the Hudson River into New Jersey. To Howe's frustration, Washington refused to be cornered or maneuvered into a showdown fight. Such evasive tactics might prevent complete defeat, but as the Americans fell back toward the Delaware River, desertions ran high and the army shrank as if it had suffered heavy losses in battle. Washington was now in command of only about 3,000 discouraged men.

The first victories

Howe, always slow to move, this time did not bother to give personal pursuit. New York society and his low regard for Washington's raggletaggle army prompted him to turn over the chase to Cornwallis, who quickly sent the Americans flying into

Pennsylvania. Philadelphia was now vulnerable, and on December 12, Congress, fearful of capture, fled, to take up temporary quarters at Baltimore. Only two days before, Congress had issued resolutions expressing great confidence in the cause and enjoining its supporters to stand firm in these critical hours. Philadelphia was not a great military base, but the damage its capture would have upon American morale was incalculable. Washington was now faced with the necessity of gaining even a small success, for clearly the military and political situation was deteriorating. Such was the background for his now-famous crossing of the Delaware River on Christmas night. He attacked the celebration-spent Hessian mercenaries at Trenton, New Jersey, early the following morning. The casualties were low, about 30 British and five Americans, but the total of prisoners ran to about 900 men and officers. To raise the spirits of the Philadelphians—and all Americans—Washington marched his Hessian prisoners through the streets of Philadelphia, and almost precipitated a riot among the citizenry, who wanted prompt revenge. The action at Trenton was no more than a raid—the American troops drank too much of their booty to keep on fighting—but it indicated to both sides that the ragged rebels had not yet given up.

Washington now had to prove to the enemy—and to his countrymen—that the successful attack upon the sleepy Hessians had been more than a

Dividing the colonies

Holding to the original plan of dividing the colonies and subduing them one by one, the British now proposed to send about 7,000 men under General John "Gentleman Johnny" Burgoyne from Quebec to Albany, by way of Lake Champlain. Howe would then send a force from New York City to meet him, thus closing the nutcracker on the Americans. Lord Germain, colonial secretary, had made it a practice to cut Howe's requests for men and supplies, but in his enthusiasm for the new campaign, he was lavish in his support of Burgoyne's army. The campaign was so widely publicized that even the Americans knew all about it. Down out of Canada marched the British, striking the Americans hard at Ticonderoga, where they won decisively. Confident now, with his splendidly equipped troops and his brilliantly hued Indian allies as outriders, Burgoyne pressed on toward Albany, where he hoped to join Howe's forces.

Howe did not share Germain's high optimism for Burgoyne's campaign. He had no objection to a pincers movement and in fact had long advocated it, but he was annoyed because Burgoyne had received reinforcements that Howe himself wanted. Lured by reports of loyalist strength in Pennsylvania, he moved his army there from New York in July, 1777, determined to strike a master blow that would split the colonies in two and end the war. With elaborate caution he approached Philadelphia, denied to him the year before, hoping to crush Washington's army while he captured the city. But try as he would, Howe could not catch the elusive Washington or lure him into battle, and the lost time foreclosed the possibility of joining Burgoyne up the Hudson River.

By September, Burgoyne approached Albany, where General Horatio Gates awaited him in a strong defensive position on the banks of the Hudson. Burgoyne's forces had dwindled. About 15,000 of his men had been left behind to guard Fort Ticonderoga; another 800 had been lost in a sharp action at Bennington, Vermont. Only about 5,500 remained. Meanwhile, word sped across the countryside of Burgoyne's progress, and as he drew on, American militiamen —ill-equipped and variously armed— appeared from everywhere. By the end of September, they outnumbered the British about three to one.

The fall rains turned roads into mire, and Burgoyne's army bogged down. Nevertheless, he attacked, believing it to be his only hope, as each day increased the disparity in size of the two armies. In a series of actions around Saratoga, in which the Americans counterattacked heavily, the British lost some 600 men. Failing to get the expected support from Howe, and unable to retreat, Burgoyne surrendered his entire force, still nearly 5,000 strong. He tried to take some of the sting out of the defeat by calling his capitulation a "convention"—a condition of which was that his men, after pledging they would not again serve in the American campaign, would be marched to Boston and given passage home. Burgoyne's suspicions were aroused by the alacrity with which Gates accepted this condition, but there was nothing he could do but sign and take his chances. He lost his gamble, for Congress refused to support the promise of parole and held the prisoners on this side of the Atlantic until the war's end.

Climax

The victory at Saratoga by the Continental Army prevented the British from driving a wedge between the colonies. And it showed that American troops could beat British troops. The French observed this battle with particular interest—as they had observed Washington's defeats in 1777 at Brandywine Creek and at Germantown in Pennsylvania, and the British settling down for the winter in Philadelphia. Historians argue over how much influence Saratoga had on the French decision to aid America, but no one denies that it had some. It now appeared that the Americans had a better-than-even chance to win their war. More than that, France knew the British were in a conciliatory mood,

ready to offer attractive peace terms. If this happened, the British would be strong again. After weighing these considerations, the French invited Benjamin Franklin and Silas Deane to a conference. During February and March, 1778, arrangements were worked out whereby France and the American colonies would make common cause against England. It was agreed that neither would make a separate peace with the enemy. Along with the war treaty, another was made

In the battle of Germantown, Wayne and Sullivan lead the American forces, in the background, against the British, who took refuge in the Chew House (right). The 1782 painting is by Xavier Della Gatta.

VALLEY FORGE HISTORICAL SOCIETY

220

between France and America, providing for commercial friendship and cooperation. The importance of the French alliance is hard to overestimate. Without it, the outcome of the American Revolution might have been far different.

In June, 1778, France formally entered the war on the American side. The next year, Spain joined as an ally of France. Holland then declared war on England, and in 1780, the Continental nations formed the League of Armed Neutrality. Its members—Denmark, Sweden, Russia, Prussia, Holland, Portugal, and Austria—were tired of England's interpretations of her privileges on the seas and were ready to fight. It is not hard to understand why Englishmen began to lose interest in the American conflict. With France, Holland, and Spain at war with her, with an armed league bristling with threats, and with military reverses across the Atlantic, England asked for negotiations.

In 1778, even before Spain had joined France against England, five commissioners had been appointed by Parliament to talk with the Americans about a settlement. They had been empowered to offer almost anything—except independence. The Earl of Carlisle, who headed the mission, had been obliged to report to Parliament that the Americans were not interested in his terms. Now, in 1780, a French army of 5,000 veterans, ready to fight alongside their allies, reached Rhode Island. The British, who still hoped to negotiate, nevertheless continued their military efforts, and turned again toward the Southern states. Trying to drive a wedge there, they succeeded in cutting off Georgia. And in May, 1780, they captured Charleston. Gates was dispatched to drive them out, but he was roundly defeated.

Before long, however, Americans had better news. Cornwallis, hoping to lead his troops through Virginia and cut the colonies in two, landed a large force at Yorktown on the York River. By August, 1781, with French naval forces blocking his retreat by sea, and French and American soldiers surrounding his fortifications, he was cornered. On October 19, he surrendered his entire army of 7,000 men, and the British government, thor-

oughly discouraged by the turn of events, hastened to sue for peace.

The naval war

While American land forces struggled against the enemy on the battlefield, and public lethargy at home, a young and untried navy did its best to cope with overwhelming odds at sea. Its beginnings were as informal as those of the Continental Army, of which the colonies' first armed vessels were a part. But in the fall of 1775, Congress decided that naval warfare should be under the control of the Marine, or Naval, Committee. A sum of $100,000 was appropriated for the outfitting and manning of ships. To encourage enlistment, men and officers were promised half the profits from captured prizes.

The regular navy was never large. It consisted of about 40 deep-water "principal ships," plus a smaller num-

On October 17, 1781, exactly four years after Burgoyne's surrender at Saratoga, Cornwallis wrote to Washington asking for a cease-fire, "to settle terms for the surrender of the posts of York and Gloucester." Frenchman Louis Van Blarenberghe, an eyewitness at Yorktown, painted the long, thin column of white-uniformed French troops marching into the siege lines around Yorktown as officers (center) make plans.

The British Serapis *(right) is raked by the* Bonhomme Richard *during the battle fought in 1779 by John Paul Jones (above).*

ber in the fresh-water fleet on the Great Lakes. By the end of the war, only three first-line vessels remained; the others had all been sunk or captured. American privateers, with their rapierlike thrusts at British commerce, were the most effective sea force. Through his daring exploits, which included raids on England and Ireland, John Paul Jones became the hero of this war. The battle between his *Bonhomme Richard* (named in honor of Benjamin Franklin) and the British *Serapis* was to become a highlight in American naval legend. Although Jones lost his own ship, he captured the *Serapis* and sailed it into a French port. Through the efforts of Jones, Captain John Barry, and others, some 200 enemy vessels were taken. Besides crippling the British fleet, the Americans got from these

prizes some $6,000,000 worth of much-needed supplies. The harassment at sea was long remembered by Great Britain, and Americans were to use the same weapon to advantage again in their next war with her.

Peace at any price

Before Yorktown, it is doubtful if the Americans could have had peace without allowing the British to retain the territory they had already captured. The royal navy held most of the important seaports from New York to Savannah. But Yorktown was such a blow that Lord North resigned in despair. George III wrote a statement of abdication, thought better of it, and asked Lord Rockingham to form a new government and try for peace. With men friendly to the Americans in control, the official British attitude changed. When Benjamin Franklin was approached in Paris, he sensed that his position was much improved and stipulated complete independence, including return of captured territory. (He also blandly asked for all of Canada, suggesting that American ownership would prevent later difficulties, but the request was later dropped.)

Lord Shelburne, who became prime minister in July, 1782, was a statesman of vision and willing to negotiate. The American commissioners proceeded to deal with him—despite their promise to the French that they would not sign a separate peace—and on November 3, 1782, terms were agreed upon. A proviso was included that the treaty would not go into effect until England and France signed articles of peace. When that was done, in January, 1783, the American Revolution was in reality over.

The terms of the final treaty, signed September 3, 1783, refute the 20th-century belief that America never lost a war or won a peace. The young nation gained its freedom, and lands east of the Mississippi River as well. Thanks to the wily New Englander, John Adams, fishing rights in Canadian waters, previously granted to the colonies, were retained. The British further promised not to carry off any American property when they evacuated their forces, and asked in return that debts owed to British subjects by Americans be paid. Our commissioners said they would recommend payment and not hinder collection—an evasively vague commitment, as later developments proved.

With the war over, the peace signed, and George III on record as having said good riddance, the Americans were free to embark upon the seas of independence. The next few years were to indicate that the waters of freedom are often choppy and the responsibility of operating the ship of state much greater than can be foreseen. But, for better or for worse, the colonials had struck out for themselves; now they would have only themselves to answer to for future mistakes. This was the way they wanted it.

SPECIAL PICTURE PORTFOLIO

THE ARMS
AND THE MEN

The American Revolution was an 18th-century war, fought in the style of that time. The battlefields were cloaked in the smoke of cannons, the air heavy with the sharp smell of black powder. Drums beat as the troops advanced, and the neighing of wounded horses filled the air. The colonials were ill-prepared at the start, fighting without experienced officers, organization, ammunition, or uniforms, but they gained experience and equipment as battle followed battle. Fortunately, they began their revolt when Britain's military commitments overseas were already high and her supply of adequately trained manpower was low. But the British, with their long tradition of military excellence and superior equipment, were still formidable enemies. The Revolution was an infantryman's war, and this gave the colonials another advantage: They were defending their own country and fighting in their own fields, while most of the British troops were strangers to the land. Although the American infantryman was not so well trained in the manual of arms as the British, he had usually hunted for his livelihood in frontier country and could handle a rifle or musket well. Moreover, he often carried his own familiar weapons into battle. By the end of the war the American army had improved its organization and effectiveness, but it soon dispersed, the farmers and merchants returning to their occupations. Created for a specific purpose, there was no longer any need for it to remain active.

227

GUILFORD COURTHOUSE NATIONAL MILITARY PARK

MARCH TO BATTLE

Both British and American troops marched into the battles of the Revolution to the rhythm of drums like the one at the left.

As *Recruiting Serjeant,* the satirical drawing at the right illustrates, the British found it hard to get good recruits.

The flintlock musket was the standard infantry weapon in the Revolution. The drawings below, published in a British drill manual, show (1) the musket, (2) the bayonet being affixed, (3) the musket being primed and loaded, (4) the bayonet charge, and (5) the musket being fired.

1

2

3

5

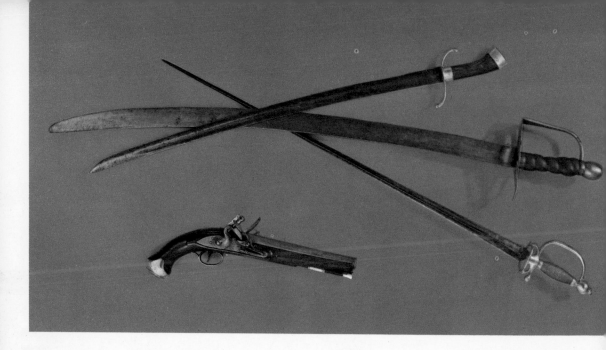

Swords and pistols were used in the Revolution as well as muskets. The British pistol was carried by a cavalryman. The hunting sword (top) and the small sword (bottom) were carried by officers; the heavy weapon at center is a cavalry saber.

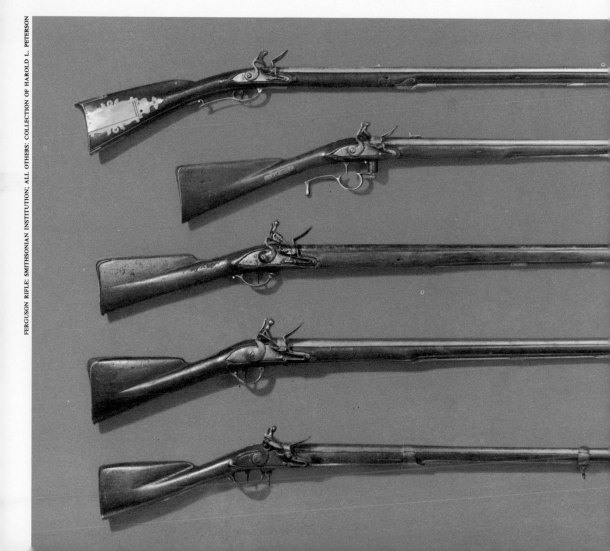

THE INSTRUMENTS OF WAR

The weapons above, used on Revolutionary battle-fields, are (top to bottom) bayonets, a tomahawk, a spontoon, and a halberd. Tomahawks were carried by American troops; spontoons on poles were used in charges; and the halberd was a symbol of rank.

Rifles and muskets of the Revolution (left, top to bottom) are the American rifle (also called the Kentucky rifle or the Pennsylvania rifle), the Ferguson rifle, a Committee of Safety musket, a Brown Bess musket, and a French infantry musket.

231

CANNON
AND MORTAR

The drawings of cannon and mortar below were published in Muller's *Treatise of Artillery*. Above is a cannon drawn by Charles W. Peale in his diary.

So desperate was the colonists' need for cannon that 59 were dragged by oxen through the snow from the captured British fort at Ticonderoga to Boston.

233

WEST POINT MUSEUM, FORT TICONDEROGA MUSEUM, WASHINGTON'S HEADQUARTERS AND MUSEUM, COLLECTION OF H. CHARLES MCBARRON—PHOTO, ARNOLD NEWMAN

THE ARMS AND THE MEN

A SOLDIER'S GEAR

Assembled here are uniforms and equipment of American infantrymen, including canteen, pipe, money, maps, and red blanket roll. The coat, buff vest, and pants, buckled shoes, and plumed cap (far right) were worn by the Continental Corps of Light Infantry in 1780. The infantryman carried the French musket with bayonet (top), and he made his own cartridge for it from paper, black powder, and lead ball (on vest). The rifleman wore a spun linen shirt and tricorn hat (far left) and carried a powder horn, lead balls, and shot pouch (on shirt) instead of cartridges; riflemen also carried tomahawks (top).

BATTLE DRESS

BOTH: COLLECTION OF MRS. JOHN NICHOLAS BROWN

The two views of an American rifleman (left and above), taken from a German engraving made in 1775, were based on drawings of a Bavarian officer who had served with the British. This colonial put together his uniform from his hunting clothes, for in the early years of the Revolution no uniforms were issued.

The Continental Army eventually acquired regulation dress (left), purchased in France and adopted toward the end of the Revolution.

The appearance of the rebel rifleman (right) is caricatured by a British artist.

Some American rebels dressed like those in the engraving below. Many Continentals, the German artist had been told, were barefoot.

REGIMENTAL FLAG, 5TH FOOT

HIS MAJESTY'S ARMY

REGIMENTAL FLAG, 33RD FOOT

REGIMENTAL FLAG, 9TH FOOT

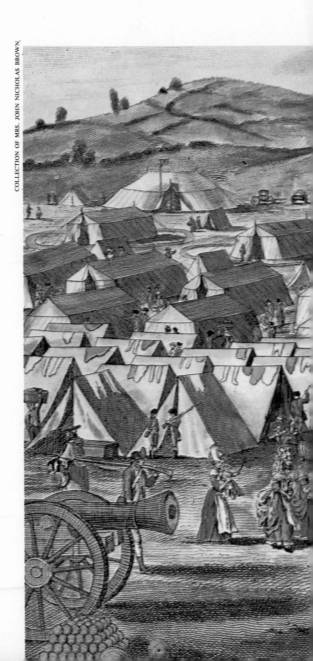

Wherever the British army went, it took its historic uniforms and ancient traditions. The man at the right is an 18th-century grenadier officer; to his right is a drummer boy in full dress.

The British army established many camps in the colonies like the one below. These tent cities were laid out in a traditional pattern and were run according to a long-established set of regulations, enforced by experienced career officers.

BRITISH MUSEUM, LONDON

AID FROM ABROAD

The Continental Army eagerly enlisted the support of Europeans. King Louis XVI of France sent four superbly trained and equipped infantry regiments to fight beside the rebels. They were dressed like the men in the print by an 18-century French artist (opposite). Rochambeau, the general the French sent to America, is shown drilling his troops in the cartoon above, by the British artist Thomas Colley, which makes fun of the elegant soldiers.

The German soldier at the left was one of the 30,000 German mercenaries who fought for the British in the colonies. As many of the men were from the state of Hesse-Cassels, they were called Hessians.

SOISSONNOIS.
LIMOSIN. BRETAGNE.

THE ARMS AND THE MEN

THE BATTLE OF PRINCETON

One of the great American victories of the Revolution was the defeat of the British in Princeton on January 3, 1777. This view of the battle was painted by the son of the American general, Hugh Mercer, who was mortally wounded there. George Washington (on horseback, left center) is directing American cannon fire with his sword. The British army is massed beyond the fence at the far right. In the first state of the battle, fought in William Clark's orchard south of Princeton, the advance guard of the Americans met British troops headed toward Trenton to join General Cornwallis. The British were winning the confused melee—until Washington arrived with the main force of his American troops and succeeded in forcing the British to retreat to New Brunswick.

Painted in the early 1800s by John A. Woodside of Philadelphia, this patriotic composition expresses the feelings of the new nation's youthful independence.

CHAPTER 9

REVOLUTION WITHIN

During the war years, the sound and fury of battle reflected the more dramatic, overt aspects of the American Revolution. Equally significant was the revolution taking place at the same time in the political, social, and economic life of the new Americans. Slave trade and inheritance laws, penal codes and education for all—these were just a few of the matters under discussion in state legislatures. Eighteenth-century liberalism helped to germinate seeds of liberty and democracy; the Revolution was the hothouse that nurtured them. Only when the fighting was over, and their independence won, did Americans begin to sense that a new nation had been created.

In the years between the settling of Jamestown and the signing of the Declaration of Independence, the colonial tasted independence and found he liked it. To achieve self-determination, and freedom from the mother country, he reluctantly joined in a common fight, waged by a loose confederation of states. To this confederation he gave only mild allegiance; his strong loyalty was to his own state. The ardently patriotic New Yorker or Virginian seemed hardly aware that what had influenced him might have had the same effect on his neighbor. Each state regarded itself defiantly and proudly as a separate, self-sufficient entity, and had no intention of relinquishing the sovereignty it was struggling to wrest from England to a strong central government, even if it helped form it. One by one, each state set about establishing its own government.

The colony becomes a state

The people, as John Adams said, wanted "a standing law to live by." This demand of the American for written law had its beginnings many years before. Colonies had been founded under written charters; they had been governed by them through the colonial years. With faith that their cause would triumph, 11 of the 13 colonies put their most respected citizens to drafting a constitution for their state, which they expected to be the supreme law of the land.

What were the sources of these state constitutions? What influenced them? In what way were they alike? From the 18th-century political theorists, such as John Locke, the constitution-makers adapted the fundamental yet revolutionary belief that all power is derived from the people, who will govern themselves through duly appointed representatives or officials. (And to safeguard their republican governments, the constitutions provided checks and balances.) From England, the constitution-makers borrowed the common law, under which the colonists had lived for many years. They also retained many elements of colonial political institutions, all of which had originally derived from British forms of government. Out of this common background

of ideals and political experience, each state drew up a constitution that was, as we shall see, much like that of its neighbor.

In detail, the constitutions varied widely. For example, Virginia's, drafted in 1776, had features familiar to modern Americans. It had three parts—a Bill of Rights, a Declaration of Independence, and a Frame of Government. In good Jeffersonian language, the document stated that all men are created equal, and all power is derived from the people, who can change their form of government when they change their minds. The Frame of Government, containing 21 parts, set up a bicameral legislature and provided for the election of a governor by joint ballot of both houses.

Pennsylvania's constitution, also drafted in 1776, was more radical. It was fathered by Benjamin Franklin, but those who deeply feared executive power apparently gained control of the convention. The legislature was to be a single house; every free man who had lived and paid taxes in Pennsylvania for a year could vote; an executive council ruled in place of a governor. The supremacy of the legislative branch was emphasized by the ruling that the executive council could not veto any act of the legislature. This did not mean that the legislators could run free, however. A council of censors, elected every seven years, was to see to it that the constitution was not violated. Although they could not actually annul laws, they were em-

Samuel Adams, painted by John Singleton Copley, was a member of the Massachusetts constitutional convention held in 1780.

powered to request a constitutional convention to amend the constitution, and this power was an impressive deterrent to unruly legislators.

The Massachusetts constitution, drafted in 1780, is probably the best example of a deliberate transition from colony to commonwealth. With minor modifications it is still the fundamental law of that state. Until 1780, Massachusetts had been governed by its provincial charter. When the people learned that the General Court (a legislative body) intended to draw up a new state constitution, they objected. People from Concord, for example, were reluctant to trust the legislature with anything so important; they recommended a constitutional convention. When the General Court, ignoring the objections, issued a constitution proposed by its own members, five-sixths of the voters said no. Smarting under the defeat, the General Court had to call a convention.

At the convention, a committee that included John Adams was appointed to draft a new constitution. Its work was accepted and adopted on March 2, 1780. Elaborate safeguards to protect the individual were included. Here, unlike Pennsylvania, men of substance were powerful enough to make sure that radical democracy was not triumphant. Relatively high property qualifications for voting and officeholding guaranteed that the "right" people would rule.

The constitutions reveal, like all compacts resulting from compromise,

Jefferson contributed to Virginia's constitution. Painted by Rembrandt Peale.

the conflict between the far left and the far right. Usually the conservatives were able to get an early advantage, and the most influential members of society saw to it that their property interests were protected.

In Pennsylvania the middle classes and the frontiersmen gained control of the revolutionary movement, and as a result the constitution was liberal. Western Pennsylvanians won equal representation with the eastern Pennsylvanians, something not accomplished in all states. In Virginia, where the conservatives were able to dominate the liberals, the constitution was middle-of-the-road. South Carolina's, drafted in 1778, was so conservative that it made Virginia's look liberal. It

247

James Wilson, member of the Pennsylvania convention in 1776 and the Continental Congress, believed that the sovereignty of a government must reside in the people.

limited suffrage to men owning at least 50 acres of land. To hold office, a man had to have much more: A senator had to be worth at least 2,000 pounds, a governor had to have 10,000. Because of loose voting regulations, rich Charleston residents could be elected to represent areas in which they held land. Thus, about one-fifth of the people in South Carolina ruled the other four-fifths. The wealthy coastal planters were a stronghold of conservatism that dominated South Carolina through the Civil War.

Land the equalizer

Property qualifications did not, however, create a strong ruling class. Tradesmen and artisans who lived in towns usually had to suffer second-class citizenship. But most of the dominant group—90% of them—lived by tilling the soil. Farmers with little or no land could reasonably expect to become substantial property owners. The war itself brought about a tremendous turnover in ownership. With the restrictions of 1763 invalidated, the colonial had access to the limitless acres beyond the Appalachians. Along the Atlantic seaboard, land from individual and crown holdings was redistributed.

Proprietary landholders suffered under the revolutionaries. Pennsylvania helped itself to the unassigned lands of the Penn family, valued at about 1,000,000 pounds, granting the family only 130,000 pounds "in remembrance of the enterprising spirit of the founder." In Maryland the "remembrance" was a mere 10,000 pounds, so small that the British government later contributed an additional 90,000 pounds. The holdings of Lord Thomas Fairfax in Virginia, 5,000,000 acres, were confiscated by the state after his death in 1781.

Loyalists were deprived of their

holdings in all possible ways. Some large private estates, abandoned by Tories, were divided and sold. As the Revolution dragged on, the bitterness of the patriots increased. By 1778, wholesale confiscation of property was common. The loyalists were fined for evading military duty, for harboring the enemy, and for countless minor infractions. They were taxed unreasonably. Although forced to accept rents in depreciated Continental currency, they had to pay their own expenses and debts with hard money. In South Carolina and New York they were held responsible for robberies in their neighborhoods. The high point came in November, 1777, when the Continental Congress suggested that the states sell the property held by those believed to be loyal to the king and invest the money in Continental loan certificates. Within three years every state but South Carolina had.

In these ways, more and more land fell into the hands of patriots, many

More and more in the late years of the 18th century, emigrants moved along the Great Philadelphia Wagon Road and other trails leading west, filling the Appalachian slopes with farms like this one. Painted in 1845 by Edward Hicks.

of whom had never owned any before. Here we see the Revolution in a more revolutionary light. It had begun as a civil war between two parts of the Empire, but it developed into a political and economic struggle between the ruling class and the newly emerging class. The landed aristocracy lost much of its power as the new land-owners expressed their will at the ballot box. At a stroke they were elevated socially, politically, and economically. They did not mind paying taxes instead of quitrents, for they expected in return, and got, services from the state.

As the new land titles deluged the earlier aristocrats, their position was gradually washed away. Jefferson himself led the assault upon such feudal vestiges as the laws designed to preserve estates intact, which forbade their division. Other states followed Virginia, and by 1800 all states but two had decreed that *all* heirs had to get a share of the property at the death of the owner. Thus primogeniture, which gave the entire holding to the oldest son, and entail, which forbade dividing an estate, were virtually outlawed. (In North Carolina, daughters could not inherit property when there were sons in the family. In New Jersey, daughters were allotted a half portion.) The attack upon land monopoly was so widespread that when the Frenchman Alexis de Tocqueville visited the United States in the 1830s, he commented that the radical inheritance laws were partially responsible

for the existence of democracy. He maintained that keeping estates intact is necessary for an aristocracy.

Other equalizers

Land distribution was the core of the revolution within. It widened suffrage, which in turn enabled democratic-minded men to strike out at all kinds of social injustice.

In a number of states the Anglican church had long stood as a symbol of British authority. It was the official dispenser of religious dogma—and worse, in the eyes of many, were the taxes levied upon all for its support. As early as 1776, the new state constitutions of Maryland and North Carolina took from the Anglican church its privileges, and Virginia followed. Jefferson, who headed the fight, described it as "the severest in which I have ever been engaged." Other states, like New York, Georgia, and South Carolina, took a less direct approach. Freedom was granted to all sects, thus depriving the Anglican church of its privileged position as the state church. It was left to compete with the others on equal terms. If it survived, the states had no particular objection. Such reforms were received with joy by such sects as the Baptists, who claimed they had been subjected to "spiritual tyranny" by both the Anglican church and New England Congregationalism.

The increasing feeling that human slavery had no place in the new order began to grow strong. How could the

Daniel Boone leads a group of pioneers west through the mountain passage that was known as the Cumberland Gap. Painting is by George Caleb Bingham.

American trumpet about the rights of man when there were a half-million slaves in the 13 states? Patrick Henry, with his keen awareness of injustice, said, "I believe a time will come when an opportunity will be offered to abol- ish this lamentable evil." Nor was this Virginian the only one who objected. In 1774, the First Continental Con- gress heard discussions of slavery as a wrong that should be corrected, and it adopted a nonimportation agree-

The French Revolution began in 1789. In part inspired by what had taken place in America, it also resulted from the excesses of the French kings, such as in building the Palace of Versailles (right).

ment on slaves. That same year the legislature of Rhode Island recorded its sentiment that personal liberty was the right of all men, regardless of color. Some states actually passed legislation against the slave trade; others sought to undermine it with prohibitive duties.

Slavery was only one of the social problems under review. Imprisonment as a penalty for unpaid debts was abolished, and many an honest man who had become financially enmeshed was given the opportunity to redeem himself. The number of offenses punishable by death was sharply cut back. An interest in general education emerged, and Pennsylvania and Virginia worked to establish public schools. Again Jefferson led the fight in Virginia, contending that a certain amount of state-financed education should be available to all men. Himself a man of some means, he nevertheless opposed fervently an aristocracy based upon wealth.

The struggle for union

Common danger during the war was what moved the colonies toward confederation. But the concept of a United States of America had existed, however weakly, long before the Revolution. Political theorists and even imperial administrators had cherished the dream of unity along the Atlantic frontier, but colonial jealousies had thus far prevented it. From time to time, events had drawn the colonies into thoughts of union. In 1643, Massachusetts, Plymouth, Connecticut, and New Haven had formed the New England Confederation. Again, in 1754, Benjamin Franklin drew up the

Albany Plan of Union, which would unite all the colonies (except Georgia and Nova Scotia) under one president general. Both efforts resulted from Indian problems. The Confederation was terminated in 1684; the Albany Plan of Union was rejected outright by the colonies as well as by the English government.

In July, 1775, Franklin presented the idea of union to the Continental Congress. At that time there was little talk of independence, and his plan made no mention of it. He recommended a United Colonies of North America, formed for friendship and common defense. Each colony would have jurisdiction within its own boundary, and a general congress would handle all external affairs.

Given broad powers, the congress would act in the interest of general welfare and would try to settle differences between individual colonies. Matters best handled jointly—postal services, the regulation of currency, the control of commerce— would fall within its province. Each member colony would be expected to help financially and would be represented in the congress according to its male population. In place of a head of state, the united colonies would be governed by a board of councilors.

Many agreed with Franklin that unity was necessary. A decade before, a Charleston resident had written, "There ought to be no New England men, no New Yorkers, etc., known on the continent, but all of us Americans." Patrick Henry said it another way in 1774: "Where are your landmarks, your boundaries of Colonies . . . I am not Virginian, but an American." Yet even as late as 1776, when the Declaration of Independence was being drawn up and a committee had been appointed to consider a national constitution, delegates to the Continental Congress were still contesting the merits of the tentative provision that the central government would arbitrate boundary disputes.

The suggestion that each state have a single vote, and yet be taxed according to population, aroused even more vigorous protest, especially from the Southerners. They did not want Negroes counted for tax purposes, claiming that slaves were simply property and should no more be taxed than sheep or cattle. (This debate was held within four weeks of the adoption of the Declaration of Independence, which proclaims the equality of men!)

Franklin opposed a single vote for each state, maintaining that each should be represented according to the size of its population. Others differed over the question of empowering the national government to control Western lands. Georgia, the least populated of the colonies, had the most extensive land claims. Pennsylvania, one of the largest colonies, had no claims beyond her charter limits.

It is not surprising that heated debates developed over such questions. Although Americans had proclaimed to the world that they were united, this union had come about through resistance to a common enemy. Was union necessary after the enemy had been defeated? Was it feasible or desirable? Only the most forward-looking Americans, it seemed, had committed themselves irrevocably to this dream of a united America.

Government by permission

The Continental Congress should have formulated a government in 1776. That year marked the high point of nationalistic spirit during the war, and at its apex was Congress, popular and respected. By 1777, when Congress approved the Articles of Confederation, it no longer enjoyed such prestige. Reluctance to accept centralized power had again surged, and

When Charles Willson Peale painted Benjamin Franklin in 1789, a year before his death, he and his country had seen revolution, independence, and—now—union.

the tide of nationalism now receded. As it was, the Articles of Confederation granted little sovereignty to the central government; herein lay their weakness. The states had reserved to themselves this requisite of an effective government. Until they agreed to relinquish at least part of it, they were participants in nothing more than a league of friendship.

The Articles, sent out to the states in the fall of 1777 for ratification, pledged "perpetual union" for common defense and for the general welfare, but it was hardly more than a hopeful sentiment. One outstanding weakness was that Congress was not granted taxing powers; this was reserved strictly to the states. Each of them was to contribute according to the valuation of its surveyed lands and buildings. Even worse, Congress was given no authority to enforce collection, and the central government was obliged to depend upon the good faith of each state. The central government could borrow money, but with such limited money-raising resources, it was certainly a poor loan risk.

These were not the only deficiencies. Foreign affairs were supposed to fall within the province of Congress, but it could make war or negotiate for peace only when nine of the states agreed. If states fell to bickering over boundaries or Western land claims, Congress could appoint a commission to arbitrate, but it was allotted no power to appropriate any land for the United States. In the years after 1781,

when the Articles of Confederation were ratified, and the United States began its experiment of constitutional government, Congressmen began to feel like mere observers, sent by their states to listen but forbidden to act. It is not surprising that the caliber of the members declined.

Although it is easy to criticize the Articles, the astute men who wrote our first constitution should be credited with a remarkable achievement: They outlined a government—whatever its lacks—that the defiant states would accept.

From the beginning its weaknesses were apparent. Attempts to get the Articles ratified brought out familiar jealousies. The main quarrel stemmed from five of the new states having definite Western limits while the others all had extensive claims beyond the mountains. New Jersey, New Hampshire, Delaware, Rhode Island, and Maryland feared that the states with land claims would become rich and powerful enough to swallow up the smaller members of the union.

Meanwhile, with the war still on, each state tended to continue its own fight with Great Britain, raiding its neighbors for men and resources when necessary, and hoarding its own strength. One can see the truth of James Madison's assertion that the newly formed federation was "nothing more than a treaty of amity, of commerce, and of alliance, between independent and sovereign states."

The Articles of Confederation indi-

Benjamin West's painting of the preliminary peace negotiations was unfinished because the British commissioners, who were to be on the right, refused to pose.

cate that the colonies had not yet achieved insight into the building of a nation. The extreme caution used in doling out power reflected the feeling that a jump to a supergovernment was both premature and dangerous. The outcome of the life-and-death struggle with Great Britain was still doubtful, and Americans were in no mood to pass from one yoke to another. Time would bring maturity to a new people. Before long the clumsiness of their government would be brought home to them, and necessity would once more be the mother of political invention.

MAIN TEXT CONTINUES IN VOLUME 4

Washington took leave of his officers at Fraunces' Tavern on December 4, 1783, the same day the

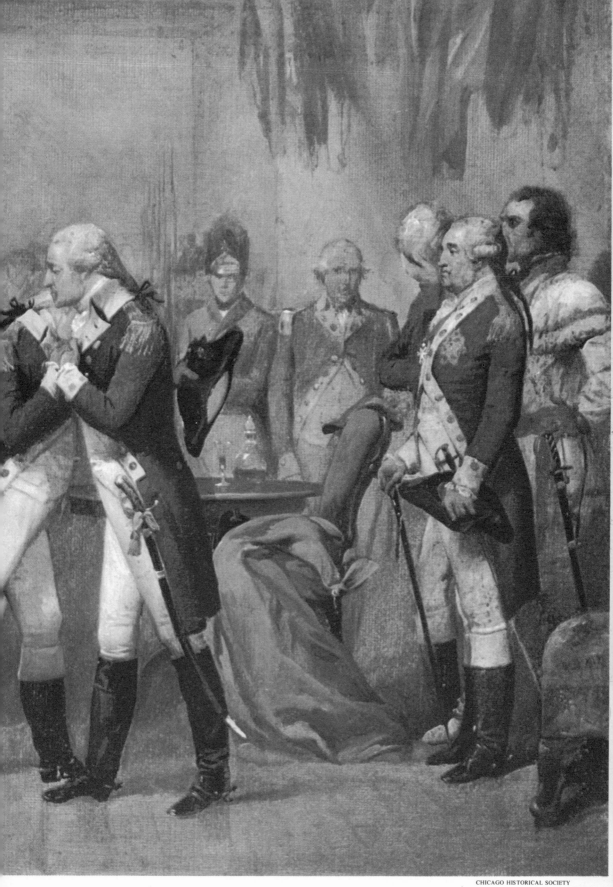

e last British troops left Staten Island and Long Island. The painting is by Alonzo Chappel.

Francis Marion (center) offers his humble meal of baked potatoes to an amazed British officer. Legend says that the artist of the painting, John Blake White, remembered Marion's features from the time he sat on his knee as a child. But as is frequently the case with the stories about the general, the whole incident may be folklore. Nonetheless, the painting was used on Confederate currency during the Civil War.

Francis Marion:
The Elusive Swamp Fox

A SPECIAL CONTRIBUTION BY
GEORGE F. SCHEER

Guerrilla warfare in South Carolina swamps and surprise attacks upon enemy regiments made this colonial general and his band of men important in winning the young nation's victory.

Our band is few, but true and tried,
Our leader frank and bold;
The British soldier trembles
When Marion's name is told.

There is the poem, there is the sentence or two in schoolbooks, and there is the sobriquet, the Swamp Fox. That's about all anyone seems to remember about General Francis Marion—except, perhaps, that once he invited a British officer to dinner, in his camp under a flag of truce, and served only fire-baked potatoes on a bark slab and a beverage of vinegar and water. "But, surely, general," the officer said, "this cannot be your usual fare." "Indeed, sir, it is," Marion replied, "and we are fortunate on this occasion, entertaining company, to have more than our usual allowance." The visiting Briton is supposed to have been so impressed that he resigned his commission and returned to England, full of sympathy for the self-sacrificing American patriots. That's not exactly the way it happened, but that's the way it goes in the Marion legend.

The legend was the invention of a specialist in hero-making, the Reverend Mason Locke

Weems. He, with the help of one of Marion's devoted soldiers, Peter Horry, wrote the first life of the general, "a celebrated partizan officer in the Revolutionary War, against the British and Tories, in South Carolina and Georgia," drawn, according to the title page, "from documents furnished by his brother-in-arms, Brigadier General P. Horry." The sensational little book, a captivating melange of fact and much fiction, firmly established Francis Marion as the Robin Hood of the Revolution.

That first "biography" appeared in 1809, and the Marion of Parson Weems remains the Marion of American history. Yet when you piece together the surviving letters, the orderly books, the official reports, you come to realize that Marion's daring forays are not merely the romantic stuff of folk literature, but that they made a definite contribution to the British defeat in the South.

From the outbreak of the Revolution until the spring of 1780, Marion put in five useful, though relatively inactive, years as an officer of the Second South Carolina Continental Regiment. But it was as a relentless guerrilla who never let up on the British after they overran his state that he earned his significance in history. He was not the only partisan those hard times discovered, but he stayed in the field longer than any of the others and best understood and carried out the mission of the partisan. And although he won no tide-turning battles, he had more than a little to do with what General Nathanael Greene, commanding the Southern Department, called "flushing the bird" that General Washington caught at Yorktown.

Marion was 48 at the time, "rather below the middle stature," one of his men recalled, "lean and swarthy. His body was well set, but his knees and ankles were badly formed . . . He had a countenance remarkably steady; his nose was aquiline, his chin projecting; his forehead was large and high, and his eyes black and piercing." It was the kind of face some men considered hard-visaged.

Marion was a man with the steady habits of a modest planter who had lived alone most of his life. He ate and drank abstemiously; his voice was light but low when he talked, and that was seldom.

Whether he fought his brigade mounted or afoot (he usually rode to the enemy and then fought as infantry), he was always in the front of the attacks that made his name a terror in the British and Tory camp. But he was not given to ferocious gesture. In fact, they say he drew his sword, a light dress weapon, so seldom that it rusted in its scabbard. It was not for personal conspicuousness in battle that his men remembered him, but for a quiet fearlessness, for sagacity and perseverance, and for never foolishly risking himself or the brigade.

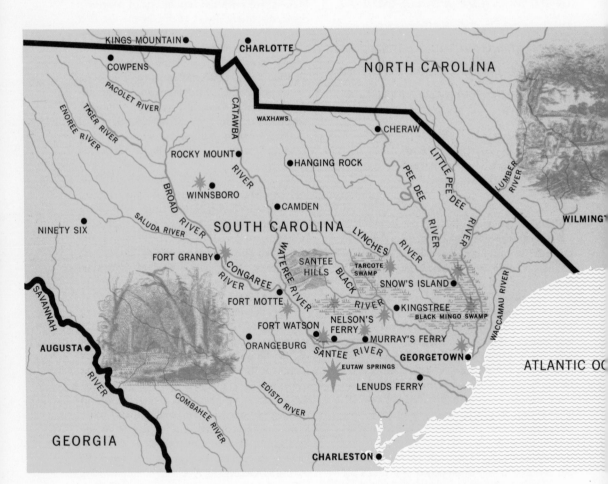

Marion's operations took place in a low, swampy region drained by many rivers, and after the Americans had been defeated at Camden, his followers represented the main colonial force in South Carolina. His major encounters with the British are marked in red.

They rode with confidence behind a man who never hesitated in the face of impossible odds to fight and run to live and fight another day. And he endeared himself to them when he slept with them on the ground, ate their fare, and endured fatigue and danger with the hardiest.

Marion's men actually had no official status. They were purely volunteers. When they came into the field, South Carolina was overrun by the British and their rebel government had evaporated. Of their own will, they took up arms to fight the invader, and it was impossible to preserve any more discipline and regularity among them than their patriotism and the dangers of the moment imposed. Fighting without pay, clothing, or provisions supplied by a government, compelled to care for their families as well as to provide for their own wants, they were likely to go home at planting or harvest time, or simply when the going got too dreary. Therefore, brigade strength fluctuated from as few as 20 or 30 men to as many as several hundred, and Marion had to plan his operations accordingly. He seldom could count on more than 150 to 200 men.

Marion's enemies charged that it was not patriotism but the appeal of plunder that held his men together. But Marion made himself clear on the subject: "Any soldier of any denomination who is found taking any article from any plantation either from white or black will be deemed a marauder & plunderer & shall suffer immediate death."

Despite their irregularities, when Marion came to disband his men in December, 1782, he could say with complete sincerity, "No citizens in the world have ever done more than they have." It was true of them. And it was true of him.

Marion was born in the country he defended to a second-generation French Huguenot family on the Cooper River in South Carolina. As a boy he lived in the vicinity of Georgetown, where he hunted and fished the salt marshes and inland swamps and semitropical woods. When he was 23 and his father, an unsuccessful planter, died, he and his mother and a brother settled for a time in upper St. John's in Berkeley County. The tradition is that he served in a mounted troop on a bootless expedition to the Cherokee country in the first flare-up of the French and Indian War on the Carolina frontier. Two years later, as a light-infantry lieutenant in a 1761 campaign against the Cherokee, he won the praise of his commanding officer as an "active, brave, and hardy soldier; and an excellent partisan officer."

Shortly before the Revolution he acquired a place of his own on the Santee River and was just getting his bachelor house in order when war came. He was elected a captain of the Second South Carolina Continental Regiment, steadily rose in Continental rank, served in the defense of Fort Sullivan in 1776 and the assault on Savannah in 1779, and for a time was in field command of the Southern Army when it wintered near the Georgia border. Through peaceful garrison times and stormy, he shared every fortune of his regiment except its last, when General Benjamin Lincoln surrendered his entire army, including the Second South Carolina, to Sir Henry Clinton at Charleston on May 12, 1780. Marion was not among the nearly 5,500 men who capitulated. For the last several weeks before the

CULVER SERVICE

The dashing Marion was idolized by his troops in much the way the legendary Robin Hood was.

fall of the city he had been convalescing at home from an ankle injury.

With Lincoln's surrender, the worst disaster the Americans had suffered in all the war, the American cause both North and South seemed all but lost. In the North, Washington's worn-out army lay deteriorating in New Jersey. The French, upon whom he had relied for reinforcements, were bottled up by a British fleet at Newport. And an enfeebled Congress and an apathetic people were allowing their rebellion to expire from sheer exhaustion. In the South, Georgia had already been occupied by the British since the winter of 1779, and within three weeks after Lincoln's surrender, South Carolina appeared to be totally subjugated. Without firing a shot, British garrisons occupied a chain of posts commanding the interior from Augusta on the Savannah River and Ninety-six on the Carolina frontier, northward to Rocky Mount, Hanging Rock, and Camden, and eastward to Cheraw and Georgetown on the coast.

To the enemy's surprise and consternation, however, the paralysis that at first seized the South Carolinians was short-lived. Lord Charles Cornwallis had hardly reported "everything wearing the face of tranquility and submission" when patriot guerrillas began a fierce, harassing warfare against him.

The partisans took some encouragement from reports that a small, new Continental army had arrived in North Carolina; around this nucleus the militia of Virginia and the Carolinas might build a force strong enough to stop the northward advance of the redcoats. In late July, when his ankle would carry him, Marion rode northward to join it with a little troop of neighbors and former army comrades. According to a Continental officer, they were "distinguished by small black leather caps and the wretchedness of their attire; their number did not exceed 20 men and boys, some white, some black, and all mounted, but most of them miserably equipped." Nevertheless, General Horatio Gates, commanding the army, recognized the value of Marion's familiarity with the country and ordered him and "the Volunteers Horse of So Carolina" to "march with and attend" him as he advanced toward the enemy's key post at Camden.

While on the march, the Marion story has it, Gates received a request from Major John James for an officer to take command of a brigade he had raised among the Scotch-Irish of Williamsburg Township on the Black River. Gates promptly assigned Marion to the command with orders to use the brigade to seize the Santee River crossings behind Camden and cut off British communication with that post and its avenue of retreat to Charleston.

Marion took command of James' brigade on Lynche's Creek about the 10th of August, 1780, and his partisan career began. After two lightning attacks on strong Tory encampments in the neighborhood, he divided his 70 men and sent a party under his old friend, Major Peter Horry, east of Lenud's Ferry on the Santee to destroy all boats and cover the crossings, while he marched westward for Murray's Ferry. After coming down on a British guard there on the night of the 23rd, scattering the redcoats and burning the ferryboats, he turned upriver toward Nelson's Ferry, 25 miles away.

Near dusk he picked up a British deserter who told him that Gates' army, upon reaching Camden, had been routed by the British on the 16th with incredible losses. From the deserter he also learned that a British escort with 150 Continental prisoners from Camden planned to rest that night at a house north of Nelson's Ferry. Without sharing with his men the depressing news of Gates' defeat, for fear they would desert him, he pushed his march all night and descended on the escort at dawn. Trapping many of the redcoats in the house, he killed two, wounded five, took 20 prisoners, and released the captured Continentals. But Marion's men heard from the prisoners that Gates had been defeated, and half of them slipped away within an hour. Marion, discovering that a heavy British patrol was in his rear, sent his prisoners toward North Carolina and retreated eastward toward the Pee Dee to make a junction with Major Horry.

Marion had no idea where the remnant of Gates' army was, or when or if it would ever be in "condition to act again." Colonel Thomas Sumter, who had bedeviled the enemy in the west, had been cut to pieces two days after the Camden debacle. Marion's little brigade was the only rebel force left intact in the state. With most of his men gone home, he now was forced after a couple of brushes with the enemy to withdraw into North Carolina.

Within two weeks, however, he had heard from Gates at Hillsboro: North Carolina was aroused, the army was putting itself back together; in South Carolina, Whig militia was assembling. Unfortunately, the Tories were gathering, too, and Gates would be pleased, he wrote, if Marion would advance to the Little Pee Dee River and disperse them. At the same time Marion heard from South Carolina that north of Georgetown the enemy had laid waste a path 70 miles long and 15 miles wide as a punishment to the inhabitants who had "joined Marion and Horry in their late incursion"; the men who had left him at Nelson's Ferry were spoiling for revenge and ready to come out again. So on a Sunday evening, the 24th of September, with only 30 or 40 men, Marion marched back into the heart of the enemy's northeasternmost defenses in South Carolina around Kingston.

The marches and actions that ensued between Marion and the British and Tories were shrewdly planned, smoothly executed, and highly damaging to the enemy. Marion brought to them not only the training of an officer of the regular service and the remembered experience of Indian-style fighting on the frontier, but also an intimate knowledge of the country. And it was the terrain that gave the native fighter a distinct advantage. It was unbelievably flat, unbelievably wet, and unbelievably wild. North and south some 80 miles from Charleston and west some 50 were its roughly figured boundaries, and down across it swept seven large rivers and many smaller ones. For miles bordering them were vast swamps. And between the swamps were the forbidding shrub bogs, spongy tangles of impenetrable vegetation. No roads crossed the swamps and bogs, except the secret paths of the hunter. But it was country that Marion

Marion and his roughly dressed men, few of whom had been issued uniforms, cross the Pee Dee River on makeshift rafts, with some of the men swimming the horses by ropes.

Major General Nathanael Greene was Marion's commanding officer. Here he is painted by Charles Willson Peale.

Colonel Henry Lee, known as Light Horse Harry, joined Marion against the British. He was also painted by Peale.

knew and understood, so for him its trails became avenues of swift surprise attack and safe retreat, its swamps and bogs his covert.

In this country during that fall of 1780, Marion's men fought at Black Mingo, northwest of Georgetown. It was another night attack, but their horses' hoofs clattering on a wooden bridge gave them away, so they lost the element of surprise and learned ever after to lay down their blankets when crossing a bridge near the enemy. They raided Georgetown, but could not draw the garrison out of the town redoubt for a stand-up fight. Another night they pounced on Tory militia at Tarcote Swamp, near the forks of Black River.

These were small engagements, but as the weeks passed into winter, Lord Cornwallis began to feel the cumulative effect of them. When Marion had retreated into North Carolina in September, Cornwallis had advanced toward Virginia as far north as Charlotte before his detached left wing had been destroyed by rebel frontiersmen at Kings Mountain, and he had

stumbled back 60 miles to Winnsboro to recover himself. In that hamlet, northwest of Camden, Cornwallis encamped for three miserable, wet months, October to January, and his letters from there make it reasonably clear that, although much of his strength had been lost at Kings Mountain and he had to await reinforcements from New York, it was the work of the partisans, especially of Marion, that tied him to Winnsboro and prevented his moving northward again.

The one man Cornwallis thought capable of running down and destroying the elusive Marion was Lieutenant Colonel Banastre Tarleton. In South Carolina, after his savage slaughter of Buford's troops at the Waxhaws, Tarleton was known as The Butcher and was without question the most bitterly hated of all the redcoats. In the British army, where his loyalist legion was famed for its energy, prowess, and daring, he had risen swiftly and at 26 was regarded as perhaps the most valuable leader of mounted troops. "I therefore sent Tarleton," Cornwallis reported, "who pursued Marion for several days, obliged his corps to take to the swamps. . . ."

There was more to it than that: Marion led Tarleton a chase in that November of 1780. Tarleton was 16 miles north of Nelson's Ferry when he discovered that Marion was a few miles south and struck out after him. About dark Marion cut through the Wood-yard, a broad and tangled swamp, and camped for the night six miles beyond it. Tarleton dared not cross the Woodyard in the dark. As he was riding around it in the morning, Marion continued down Black River 35 miles through woods and swamps and bogs, where there was no road. Tarleton, after making his way for seven hours through swamps and defiles, hit 23 miles of fair road and then ran into Ox Swamp, where the chase went out of him.

Tradition has it that when Tarleton turned back (or was called off by a courier with orders to turn about and go after Sumter in the west), he gave Marion his sobriquet: "Come on, my boys, let's go back. As for this damned old fox, the devil himself could not catch him."

For several more weeks the old fox was busily gnawing at British supply trains and posts and parties. Then, with his ammunition and supplies nearly exhausted, he took up an encampment in a romantic spot not far from the original ground of the Williamsburg men. It was called Snow's Island and was a large, high river-swamp plateau at the joining of Lynche's Creek with the Great Pee Dee. Here, deep in a forest of cypress, laurel, and pine, protected by the watercourses and tangles of canebrake and vines, he made a supply depot and rest camp that served him, off and on, for the rest of the war.

Through the rest of the winter of 1780 and into the spring of 1781, Marion played his partisan role while great events wrought great changes in the condition of the American cause in the South. In December, General Nathanael Greene arrived at Charlotte to succeed Gates in command of the Continental Army of the Southern Department. By mid-April, 1781, in perhaps the most

Banastre Tarleton, Marion's hated pursuer, was known as The Butcher. By Sir Joshua Reynolds.

267

brilliant campaign of the war, he had maneuvered a greatly weakened and confused Cornwallis into Virginia and returned to South Carolina to battle for repossession of the state.

As Greene advanced toward Camden, Marion, joined by the splendid legion of young Light Horse Harry Lee, moved against the inner chain of British posts on the Santee and Congaree. Fort Watson, their first objective, was a tremendous stockaded work crowning an ancient Indian mound that rose almost 40 feet above the surrounding plain, north of Nelson's Ferry on the Santee. When Marion and Lee failed after a week to starve out the garrison by siege, they managed to effect a surrender by firing down on the fort from a log tower, devised by a country major of Marion's brigade who probably had never heard of the warring Romans.

By May 6, when they reached Fort Motte on the Congaree, Marion and Lee had a light fieldpiece, begged from Greene's army, but it did them no good. Fort Motte consisted of a strong stockade with outer trenches and an abatis built about a handsome brick mansion on a commanding piece of ground. They spent six days digging parallels and trenches and mounting their gun, but the fieldpiece failed to make a dent in the heavy timbers of the stockade or the walls of the house. Again the attackers resorted to primitive methods. Getting up close under cover of the siege lines, a man of Marion's brigade flung ignited pitch balls on the roof, set it afire, and smoked the enemy out.

One by one the British posts fell. After repulsing Greene, the British evacuated Camden. Augusta surrendered, and Fort Granby. The British blew up their own fort at Nelson's Ferry. Marion dashed to Georgetown and this time took it. Greene himself unsuccessfully laid siege to Ninety-six, but the enemy soon evacuated it and pulled back and consolidated at Orangeburg on the Edisto. Marion, Sumter, and Lee spent a vigorous summer striking behind the enemy army, ranging almost to Charleston, while Greene refreshed his hard-marched army in the oak-and-hickory woods of the High Hills of Santee below Camden.

Late in August, Greene came down from the High Hills to fight his last pitched battle of the war, at Eutaw Springs near Nelson's Ferry, on September 8. For the first time since the assault on Savannah in 1779, Marion found himself in formal battle, in command of the right wing of Greene's front line. The whole first line was made up of North and South Carolina militia. It must have seemed strange to Marion's partisans to be there. But for once the militia did not panic; before falling back under enemy pressure, they delivered 17 rounds and wrung from Greene praise for a firmness that he said "would have graced the veterans of the great King of Prussia."

It was pretty much a drawn battle. Both sides retreated. But Greene had damaged the British so severely that soon they withdrew into their lines at Charleston and never emerged again.

Although patriots and loyalists killed one another with unrelenting bitterness for more than a year longer, the question of ultimate victory in the South was settled. On the day following the battle of Eutaw Springs, a French fleet returned to Chesapeake Bay in Virginia and sealed the fate of Cornwallis, whom Greene had driven into a faraway trap at a village called Yorktown.

In December of the next year, 1782, under the gnarled live oaks at Wadboo plantation, Marion discharged his brigade, its mission accomplished.

After the war, Marion married his cousin and lived out his last years in comfort as a small planter on the Santee. When he died in 1795, it made scarcely a stir; he was simply another old officer of the Revolution. Today many of his battle sites are hidden by towns, roads, and manmade lakes. But the old maps show where he rode and the battle documents tell what he did, and it was a magnificent performance. So perhaps it was justice, after all, that Parson Weems came along.

George F. Scheer is co-author of Rebels and Redcoats *and the editor of* Private Yankee Doodle, *a Revolutionary War soldier's autobiography. He is now general editor of the Meridian Documents of American History Series.*

FOR FURTHER READING

The American Heritage Book of the Revolution. New York: 1958. A pictorial and textual history of the American Revolution.

Beard, Charles. *An Economic Interpretation of the Constitution of the United States.* New York: Macmillan, 1925. A landmark in American historical studies.

Becker, Carl L. *The Declaration of Independence.* New York: Harcourt, Brace, 1922. This book remains one of the classic studies of the Declaration.

Bowen, Catherine Drinker. *John Adams and the American Revolution.* Boston: Little, Brown, 1950. An interesting biography of an important American patriot.

Brown, Robert E. *Charles Beard and the Constitution.* Princeton: Princeton University Press, 1956. An argument against Beard's historical methods and conclusions.

Channing, Edward. *The American Revolution, 1761–1789.* New York: Macmillan, 1923. The traditional description of government under the Articles of Confederation.

Commager, Henry Steele, and Richard B. Morris, editors. *The Spirit of 'Seventy-Six.* Indianapolis: Bobbs-Merrill, 1958. An anthology of contemporary writings on the war.

Farrand, Max. *The Fathers of the Constitution.* New Haven: Yale University Press, 1921. One of the basic studies of the Founding Fathers.

Forbes, Esther. *Paul Revere and the World He Lived In.* Boston: Houghton Mifflin, 1942. A study of Paul Revere and his times.

Gottschalk, Louis. *Lafayette Comes to America.* Chicago: University of Chicago Press, 1935. *Lafayette Joins the American Army.* Chicago: University of Chicago Press, 1937. *Lafayette and the Close of the American Revolution.* Chicago: University of Chicago Press, 1942. Three volumes on the great French general.

Greene, Evarts Boutell. *The Revolutionary Generation, 1763–1790.* New York: Macmillan, 1943. A good study of the era.

Ketchum, Richard M. *The Battle For Bunker Hill.* New York: Doubleday, 1962. An exciting account of one of the major battles.

Miller, J. C. *Sam Adams: Pioneer in Propaganda.* Boston: Little, Brown, 1936. A biography of the fiery patriot.

Morison, Samuel Eliot. *John Paul Jones, A Sailor's Biography.* Boston: Little, Brown, 1959. A biography by a fine historian of the famous naval hero. *Sources and Documents Illustrating the American Revolution, 1764–1788.* Oxford: Clarendon Press, 1923. A reference book for the documents of the Revolution.

Morris, Richard B. *The American Revolution: A Short History.* Princeton: Anvil Books (paperback), 1955. A good short history.

Namier, Sir Lewis B. *England in the Age of the American Revolution.* London: Macmillan, 1930. A study of the complexity of British politics in this period.

Nettels, Curtis P. *George Washington and American Independence.* Boston: Little, Brown, 1951. A provocative biography of the great figure of the Revolution.

Nevins, Allan. *The American States During and After the Revolution, 1775–1783.* New York: Macmillan, 1924. A study of the changes that took place in the states within this period.

Trevelyan, Sir George O. *The American Revolution.* 4 volumes. London: Longmans, Green, 1899–1913. A famous English historian writes on the Revolution.

Ward, Christopher. *The War of the Revolution,* ed. John Richard Alden. 2 volumes. New York: Macmillan, 1952. Comprehensive narrative of military operations on land.

THE AMERICAN HERITAGE NEW ILLUSTRATED HISTORY OF THE UNITED STATES

PUBLISHED BY DELL PUBLISHING CO., INC.

George T. Delacorte, Jr., *Publisher*   Helen Meyer, *President*
William F. Callahan, Jr., *Executive Vice-President*

Walter B. J. Mitchell, Jr., *Project Director;* Ross Claiborne, *Editorial Consultant;* William O'Gorman, *Editorial Assistant;* John Van Zwienen, *Art Consultant;* Rosalie Barrow, *Production Manager*

CREATED AND DESIGNED BY THE EDITORS OF AMERICAN HERITAGE MAGAZINE

James Parton, *Publisher;* Joseph J. Thorndike, Jr., *Editorial Director;* Bruce Catton, *Senior Editor;*
Oliver Jensen, *Editor;* Richard M. Ketchum, *Editor, Book Division;* Irwin Glusker, *Art Director*

ROBERT R. ENDICOTT, *Project Editor-in-Chief*

James Kraft, *Assistant Editor;* Nina Page, Evelyn H. Register, Lynn Marett, *Editorial Assistants;*
Lina Mainiero, *Copy Editor;* Murray Belsky, *Art Director;* Eleanor A. Dye, *Designer;* John Conley, *Assistant*